The Wayland Library of Science and Technology

ENERGY SOURCES

CLINT TWIST

The Wayland Library of Science and Technology

The Nature of Matter
The Universal Forces
Stars and Galaxies
The Solar System
The Changing Landscape
Air and Oceans
Origins of Life
The Science of Life
Plants and Animals
Animal Behaviour
The Human Machine
Health and Medicine

The Environment
Feeding the World
Raw Materials
Manufacturing Industry
Energy Sources
The Power Generators
Transport
Space Travel
Communications
The Computer Age
Scientific Instruments
Towards Tomorrow

Advisory Series Editor
Robin Kerrod

Consultant
Dr. J. Beynon

Editor: Caroline Sheldrick
Design: David West · Children's Book Design
Picture Research: Alison Renney
Production: Steve Elliott
Art Director: John Ridgeway
Project Director: Lawrence Clarke

First published in 1991 by
Wayland (Publishers) Ltd
61 Western Road, Hove
East Sussex BN3 1JD, England

Planned and produced by:
Andromeda Oxford Limited
The Chambers
11, 13 & 15 Vineyard
Abingdon
Oxon OX14 3PX

British Library Cataloguing in Publication Data
Twist, Clint
    Energy sources. – (Wayland library of science
    and technology)
    I. Title II. Series
    333.79

ISBN 0-7502-0067-7

Media conversion and typesetting by Peter
MacDonald, Una Macnamara and Vanessa Hersey
Origination by Hong Kong Reprohouse Co Ltd
Printed in Italy by Rotolito Lombarda
S.p.A., Milan
Bound in France by AGM

Front cover: Photovoltaic cells at the world's
largest array, at Mt. Laguna Air Force Base,
California.
Back cover: A solar panel.

Contents

Introduction

Without fuels and other sources of energy, human existence would be cold, dark and primitive. The discovery of fuel, in the form of firewood, is as old as the discovery of fire itself; but there is far too little firewood in the world to support modern civilization. At present, most of our energy comes from burning fossil fuels: coal, oil and gas. Coal is now our basic fuel; there is a plentiful supply and we have enough for hundreds of years. Oil and gas are much more useful, but we have very limited resources, enough perhaps for only another fifty years.

Twenty years ago, nuclear energy was widely believed to be the energy source of the future. Today, however, there is a large question mark over the nuclear energy industry. Attention has now turned instead to natural sources of power: solar energy, water power, wind power, wave power, tidal power and our planet's own reserves of heat energy.

◄ Solar cells, also called photovoltaic cells, produce small amounts of electricity from the energy in sunlight. Solar cells are most efficient when they are used in outer space.

Coal

Spot facts

- In the 30 years 1945-75, we burned as much coal as in all of our previous history.

- The USA has estimated coal reserves of at least three trillion (three million million) tonnes.

- A large bucket-wheel excavator can mine coal at a rate of 8,000 cubic metres per hour.

- The Yallourn Mine in South Australia contains over 13,000 million tonnes of brown coal.

- In a gas explosion in a British mine in 1951, flames travelled 12 km along the underground tunnels.

▶ Shovelling coal deep underground. Although coal mining is now highly mechanized, it still involves a great deal of human labour in very difficult conditions. In some places, coal miners have to work on their hands and knees in tunnels with a roof height of less than 1.5 metres.

Coal is a form of fossilized wood, and coalfields are the remains of great forests that existed hundreds of millions of years ago, during the Carboniferous Period. For the last two hundred years, coal has been our most important industrial fuel, and today it supplies most of our electricity. In countries where large coalfields occur, coal mining is a major industry that uses some of the world's largest machines.

Coal is our most plentiful fuel, and total reserves are enough to last for hundreds of years. Although coal mining damages the environment, and burning coal causes pollution, it is certain to remain a vital source of energy for the foreseeable future.

Fields and reserves

Coal is a black or dark-coloured mineral fuel that consists mainly of the element carbon. As well as carbon, coal contains a variety of hydrocarbons, often traces of sulphur, and moisture. Coal occurs as seams (layers in the rock strata) within the Earth's crust. The depth at which coal seams are found varies enormously. In some coalfields, the seam lies just below the surface. More often, coal seams are buried beneath hundreds of metres of rock.

The properties of coal have been known for at least 2,000 years, but coal was little used until the Industrial Revolution of the 1700s. Before then, firewood and charcoal provided virtually all the world's energy needs. During the 1700s coal quickly replaced charcoal as an industrial fuel. In the 1800s, coal provided the driving energy behind the great Age of Steam. Today, coal is used mainly to produce electricity.

▼ World coal reserves are estimated at around 10 million million tonnes. Most of them are in the Northern Hemisphere, although there are some important deposits in Australia. The USA, USSR and China between them have about 60 per cent of Earth's total resources.

Energy from coal

Total world coal production stands at about 3,800 million tonnes per year. This accounts for just less than one-third (31 per cent) of the planet's total energy production. Coal is still widely used in factory furnaces and domestic stoves, but most of the world's output is burned in power stations to produce electricity. Although it is sometimes considered an old-fashioned fuel, coal is in fact our biggest single source of electrical power, and will long continue to be so.

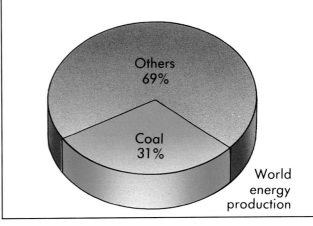

Others 69%

Coal 31%

World energy production

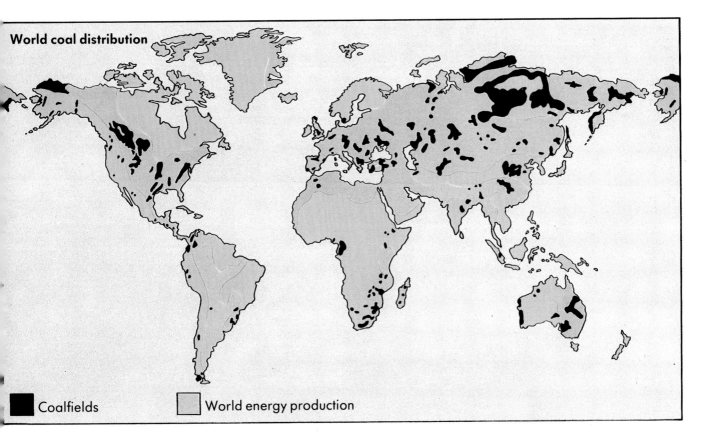

World coal distribution

■ Coalfields   ▢ World energy production

Coal formation

Coal was formed by the carbonization of trees and plants. When plants die, the carbon in their tissues is normally recycled back into the environment during decomposition. Carbonization occurs when dead plant material is subjected to heat and pressure over millions of years. The different grades of coal were formed by different combinations of time, heat and pressure.

Most of the world's coal was formed during the Carboniferous Period, between 360 and 286 million years ago. At this time, large areas of the Earth's surface were covered with dense swampy forests. Dead plants and trees that fell into the swamps did not decompose completely, but accumulated into thick layers of wet peat. When the swamps were later flooded by the sea, the peat became buried under layers of sediment. Over long periods of time, it decayed further and slowly dried and hardened into brown coal or lignite.

As further layers of sediment built up, increased heat and pressure caused lignite to turn into bituminous coal. In some instances, additional pressures turned bituminous coal into anthracite.

Anthracite and bituminous coal are known as hard coals because of their rock-like appearance. Anthracite is the best quality coal, and contains 86 to 98 per cent carbon. It burns with a bright blue flame and gives off very little smoke. Bituminous coal is the most widely occurring grade of coal, and contains 64 to 86 per cent carbon. Bituminous coal also contains the highest proportion of volatile material, which can be distilled into gas and coal tar. One of the most important discoveries of the Industrial Revolution was the process of baking bituminous coal in an oven to produce coke.

Lignite and brown coals are often referred to as soft coals, and some are soft enough to be crumbled between the fingers. They only contain about 50 to 60 per cent carbon, and are usually compressed into pellets before use.

▼ Fossil remains of the plant *Neuopteris fexuosa* found in coal. The plant lived in the Carboniferous Period (360-286 million years ago) and when the coal-forming material was laid down, it was trapped. Although the plant material decomposed, it left a clear impression in the coal seam.

▲ Coal forms where dead plant material does not properly decay. First it forms peat (1). Once buried and compressed, it becomes lignite (2). Further pressure produces bituminous coal (3) and anthracite (4). The plants were once part of swampy forests in the Carboniferous Period (left).

Nearly coal – peat

The water in swamps and bogs often does not contain enough oxygen or bacteria for normal decomposition to take place. Dead plant material slowly forms a layer of waterlogged peat. Over thousands of years, the layers build up and can reach 30 m in thickness. Although peat is still some way from being coal, it can be used as a low-grade fuel. When it is freshly cut from the ground, peat is a black slimy material containing about 70 per cent water. After it has been dried, it is a crumbly brown solid. When burned, peat gives off large quantities of thick smoke. In many rural parts of Europe, peat is still cut by hand in the traditional manner and is burned in domestic fires. In some countries it is cut by machines and used in small power stations. Most of Europe's peat reserves are now nearly depleted.

Surface mining

When a coal seam occurs just below ground level, it can be worked by surface, or opencast, mining. The overburden, the rocks and soil that cover the seam, is removed, and the exposed coal is mined by mechanical excavators.

In the simplest opencast, or open-pit, method of mining, the coal is dug mechanically out of an excavation. This is used for relatively thick seams with little overburden. For thinner seams, a widely used technique is strip mining, in which the seam is worked by cutting a series of trenches. When all the coal exposed by a particular trench has been removed, another trench is dug alongside and the overburden is used to fill the previous trench.

In Germany's Ruhr valley, the coal seam lies very close to the surface and it is only necessary to scrape aside the topsoil with draglines. In parts of the United States, however, up to 60 m of overburden lie above the coal seam.

In order to be economic, strip mining needs to be carried out on a very large scale. Some of the power shovels used can remove over 150 cubic metres of rock or coal with a single bite.

In general, it is the lower grades of coal that lie nearest the surface, and which are recovered by surface mining. This is especially true in the western United States and eastern Europe where huge deposits of brown coal and lignite are worked. Some high-quality coal is also obtained by strip mining, including almost half the anthracite produced in the United States.

The main problem with surface mining is the damage it creates to the environment, particularly if the coal lies beneath farmland. In many countries, strip mining is now carefully regulated. Some governments require that topsoil is removed and stored separately so that it may be replaced and the area replanted with the minimum of delay.

A giant walking dragline at work in a British coalfield. Draglines of this size require very large and level working surfaces in order to operate efficiently. The ordinary excavator in the foreground of the picture is dwarfed by comparison. It is used to clear obstacles from the dragline's path.

◄ An opencast coal mine in Australia, showing the extensive damage that surface mining can cause to a landscape.

► A power shovel excavator in an American strip mine. Even a very hard coal such as anthracite is soft enough to be worked by mechanical shovels and draglines. Brown coal and lignite are soft enough to be scooped out by bucket-wheel excavators.

Underground mining

▲ Typical winding gear at the pithead, often the only visible feature of a coal mine. This underground mine is in the Rhonda Valley in Wales. Early mines were not very deep and coal was carried to the surface up a series of ladders.

Underground mining is much more widespread than surface mining. Britain, for example, obtains more than 90 per cent of its coal from underground, and mines are often more than 1,000 m deep. Access to the coal seams is obtained by digging a vertical shaft. Mechanical winding gear raises and lowers cages that carry both miners and coal.

Mining is carried out along a series of horizontal tunnels and branching galleries. The exposed portion of the seam that is being worked is called the coalface. Some narrow seams (less than a metre) are still worked by hand. Thicker seams are worked by modern coal-cutting machinery that can cut up to 6,000 tonnes of coal per day.

There are two basic underground coal mining techniques: room-and-pillar and longwall. Room-and-pillar mining, which is still widely used in the United States, involves removing coal from a series of underground rooms. Large pillars of coal are left in place to support the roof of the gallery.

Rotary coal cutter

Electric train

Room-and-pillar mining

Hydraulic roof supports

Longwall coalface

Underground coal mine

▲ Modern mines have at least two shafts, one for coal, the other for miners and their equipment. A ventilation system pumps fresh air down one shaft and forces stale air out of the other. Miners may travel up to 2 km by train to the coalface. Longwall mining enables coal to be cut by rotary cutters and be carried along conveyor belts into loading hoppers. At the surface, the coal is sorted and graded according to size and quality.

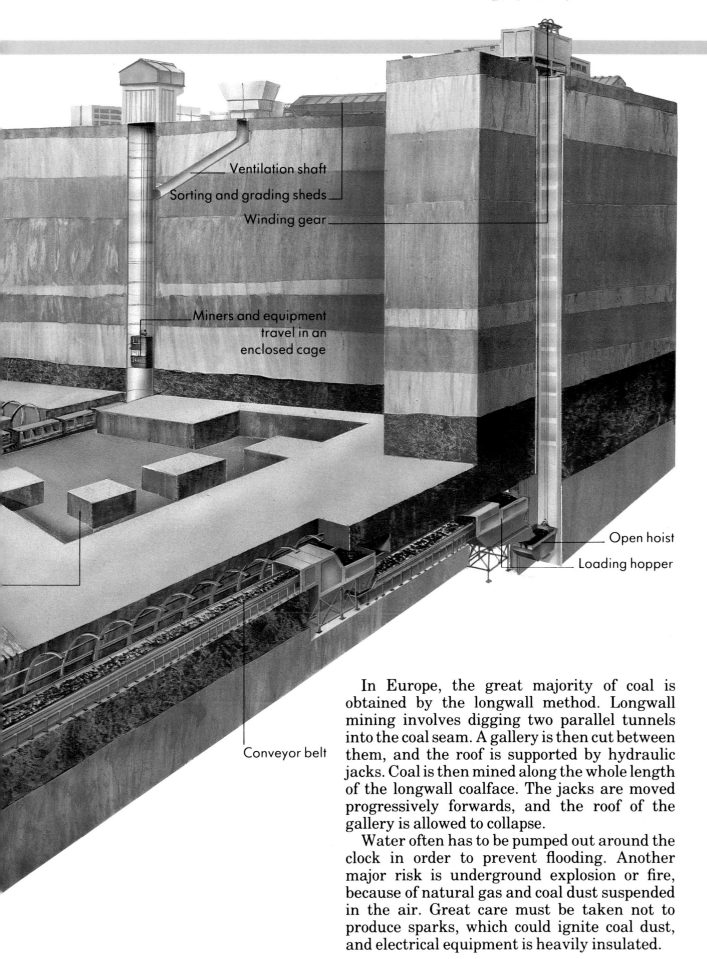

Ventilation shaft

Sorting and grading sheds

Winding gear

Miners and equipment
travel in an
enclosed cage

Open hoist

Loading hopper

Conveyor belt

In Europe, the great majority of coal is obtained by the longwall method. Longwall mining involves digging two parallel tunnels into the coal seam. A gallery is then cut between them, and the roof is supported by hydraulic jacks. Coal is then mined along the whole length of the longwall coalface. The jacks are moved progressively forwards, and the roof of the gallery is allowed to collapse.

Water often has to be pumped out around the clock in order to prevent flooding. Another major risk is underground explosion or fire, because of natural gas and coal dust suspended in the air. Great care must be taken not to produce sparks, which could ignite coal dust, and electrical equipment is heavily insulated.

13

Oil and gas

Crude oil, or petroleum, is the most valuable and the most versatile of Earth's buried treasures. Oil provides us with a number of different fuels, each of which is essential to modern civilization. Petrol, aviation fuel, diesel fuel and heating oil are all refined from crude oil. During the last 100 years, the search for oil has spread to ever more remote and difficult areas: hot deserts, offshore waters and polar wastes.

More recently, natural gas has also emerged as an important fuel, and in many parts of the world it is piped directly into houses for domestic heating and cooking. Oil and gas are frequently found together.

Fields and reserves

By weight, oil and natural gas consist almost entirely of the elements carbon and hydrogen. Chemically, these two elements are combined into thousands of different compounds known as hydrocarbons. Oil and gas occur in natural underground reservoirs that may lie thousands of metres below the surface.

Both oil and gas have been known since ancient times, but they were very little used before the 1860s. The first oil well was drilled in Pennsylvania, USA, in 1859. Within a few decades, oil had also been discovered in other countries. The most recently-developed oilfields are in the polar regions of Alaska and Siberia.

Oil has become the world's most important fuel, which, when refined, is used for domestic and industrial heating and for powering the engines of our machines. Natural gas was once considered a waste product, but is now widely exploited as a heating fuel.

▼ Total world oil reserves are estimated at around 700,000 million barrels. The largest reserves are in the Middle East, which has 26 supergiant fields. Each supergiant field contains at least 5,000 million barrels.

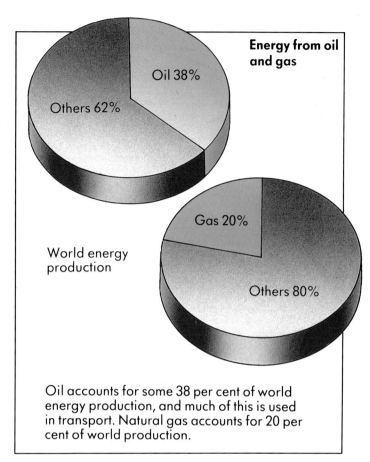

Energy from oil and gas

Oil 38%

Others 62%

World energy production

Gas 20%

Others 80%

Oil accounts for some 38 per cent of world energy production, and much of this is used in transport. Natural gas accounts for 20 per cent of world production.

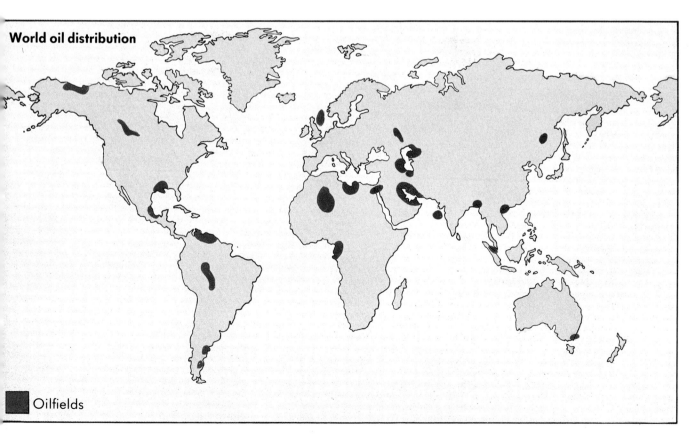

World oil distribution

■ Oilfields

Formation

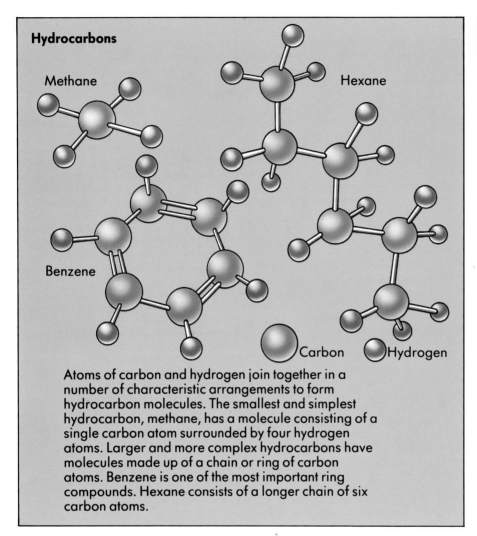

Hydrocarbons

Methane

Hexane

Benzene

Carbon   Hydrogen

Atoms of carbon and hydrogen join together in a number of characteristic arrangements to form hydrocarbon molecules. The smallest and simplest hydrocarbon, methane, has a molecule consisting of a single carbon atom surrounded by four hydrogen atoms. Larger and more complex hydrocarbons have molecules made up of a chain or ring of carbon atoms. Benzene is one of the most important ring compounds. Hexane consists of a longer chain of six carbon atoms.

▲ Pitch Lake in Trinidad, a naturally-occurring deposit that has seeped out on to the surface, forming a lake of liquid bitumen (asphalt). Bitumen is one of the heaviest hydrocarbon compounds.

Oil was formed from the remains of tiny plants and animals that lived in the oceans many millions of years ago. The exact age of oil deposits is hard to determine, because oil moves about easily and is not usually found in the rocks in which it was formed.

At some periods of Earth's geological history, the bodies of algae and plankton accumulated on the seabed and were buried under layers of sediment. The sediment preserved the organic matter from the process of decomposition. Instead, it was transformed by the action of bacteria into a substance known as kerogen. Over long periods of time, further layers of sediment produced increased temperature and pressure, which "cooked" the kerogen and produced many different hydrocarbons. Depending on the exact recipe of the "cooking", crude oil can be thick and dark, or pale and thin.

Oil is chemically stable within the Earth' crust, but a number of factors cause it t migrate physically. As a liquid, oil tends t move through the narrow spaces betwee particles of rock by capillary action. In rock tha is saturated with water, this movement i always in an upward direction because oil is les dense than water. Many oilfields are literall floating on underground water.

Like water, oil passes easily throug permeable rocks such as sandstone and limes tone, but cannot penetrate impermeable rock such as slate. Some oil deposits migrate all th way to the surface, but most are eventuall trapped by a layer of cap rock. The commones type of oil trap is an anticline, an arch in th rock strata caused by the folding of the Earth' crust. About 80 per cent of world oil productio comes from anticline deposits.

▲◄ As it migrates upwards through permeable rock, oil may become trapped by impermeable cap rock in a number of geological features: (1) an anticline, or dome; (2) a fault caused by Earth movements; (3) an incongruity (an abrupt change in the nature of the rock strata); (4) an intrusion (caused by a mass of rock pushing up from below); (5) a pinch-out (where the rock strata taper away); and (6) a salt dome (caused by the intrusion of a large pillar of rock salt).

Key
1 Anticline
2 Fault
3 Incongruity
4 Intrusion
5 Pinch-out
6 Salt dome

Natural gas is often found in association with oil, but also occurs as separate deposits. Most gas was formed by the same processes that created oil, although gas formation can take place over a wider range of geological conditions. Some gas has also been created by freshwater swamps, volcanic activity, and some has leaked from coal deposits. Gas is more mobile than oil, and may therefore migrate along different routes and be trapped in different geological formations.

The best-quality natural gas is dry gas, which consists of almost pure methane, with small amounts of ethane. Natural gas that also contains significant amounts of propane, butane and pentane is known as wet gas.

17

Production

Modern surveying techniques can predict the location of an oilfield with a fair degree of accuracy. The exact nature and value of the field has then to be proved by drilling a series of test holes to obtain samples. Only then can the location of the production wells be determined. Even on oilfields that are already in production, as many as four out of five wells that are sunk may turn out to be dry.

Under ideal conditions, natural pressure from gas and water trapped with the oil will cause it to flow up the well to the surface. Where there is no natural pressure, or where it has become exhausted, the oil must be pumped to the surface. In some cases, oil can be forced to flow up the well by pumping water into the oilfield at a different location. Other techniques, such as underground explosions, have also been used to stimulate flow from unproductive wells.

About five per cent of world oil production comes from heavy oil, which is much thicker than other crude oils. In many cases, heavy oil can only be extracted by pumping steam down the well to increase the rate of flow.

The deepest wells bring oil from more than 10,000 m underground, but many fields li within the first few thousand metres of rock Faults and layers of drill-resistant rock are much greater problem than depth. Such obs tacles can be overcome by drilling at an angle using a wedge-shaped attachment known as whipstock.

In a few countries, oil is obtained from o shales, a type of deposit in which oil is physicall locked into the rock. Brazil, Russia and Chin produce small quantities of "synthetic" crude o from oil shales. But at present the process is to expensive for large-scale production.

Undersea production

Extracting oil from beneath the seabed require specialized marine technology to overcome th additional barrier of seawater. Offshore o production began during the 1920s, but wa restricted to simple platforms on stilts built i shallow coastal waters. During the 1970s, th search for oil was extended to the deeper water of the North Sea and the Gulf of Mexico. Today oil is produced from wells drilled in up to 300 r of water.

◀ When the oil in a field is under natural pressure, the flow must be regulated by a complicated system of pipes and valves known as a "Christmas tree".

▼ The pumps used to bring up oil are often known as nodding donkeys because of their ceaseless up-and-down motion.

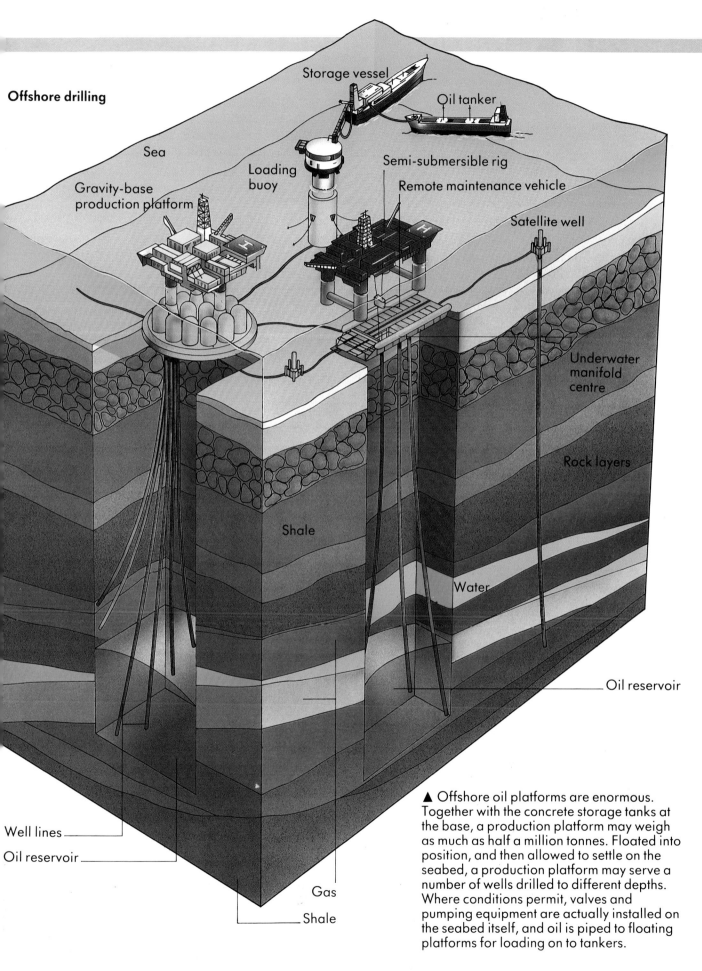

Offshore drilling

Sea

Storage vessel

Oil tanker

Gravity-base
production platform

Loading
buoy

Semi-submersible rig

Remote maintenance vehicle

Satellite well

Underwater
manifold
centre

Rock layers

Shale

Water

Oil reservoir

Well lines

Oil reservoir

Gas

Shale

▲ Offshore oil platforms are enormous.
Together with the concrete storage tanks at
the base, a production platform may weigh
as much as half a million tonnes. Floated into
position, and then allowed to settle on the
seabed, a production platform may serve a
number of wells drilled to different depths.
Where conditions permit, valves and
pumping equipment are actually installed on
the seabed itself, and oil is piped to floating
platforms for loading on to tankers.

Transportation

Transporting oil
Oil is constantly on the move, and every day about 50 million barrels are transported around the globe. The basic unit of the oil industry is the barrel, which contains 160 litres, but actual barrels are very little used today. The scale of the global trade in oil demands transportation in bulk, either by pipeline or in specially-designed ships.

The largest ships, known as supertankers or VLCCs (Very Large Crude Carriers) measure over 300 m in length, and can carry up to 3.5 million barrels of oil at a time. The oil is usually loaded and unloaded at specially-constructed deep-water ports. In some places, for example the Arabian Gulf, oil is first piped to floating platforms anchored some distance offshore. In some offshore oilfields, oil is loaded on to tankers directly from an underwater installation by a process known as well-heading. In other offshore fields, for example in the North Sea, the oil is carried from the production wells by pipelines to storage tanks onshore.

In general, pipelines are used over short distances and for local distribution. The diameter of the pipe varies between 20 and 120 cm, depending on the volume to be carried. The construction of long-distance pipelines can present tremendous engineering problems. Where these problems can be overcome, however, pipelines offer the cheapest form of bulk transportation.

One of the most demanding pipeline projects ever undertaken was the Trans-Alaskan Pipeline. It was built to transport crude oil from Prudhoe Bay in the Arctic, south to the ice-free port of Valdez. During construction, engineers had to brave blizzards and temperatures down to −50°C. They had to cross countless rivers, deal with the problem of permafrost, or permanently frozen ground, and allow for possible earthquakes and migrating herds of caribou.

▼ A liquefied petroleum gas tanker unloading its cargo into storage tanks. Natural gas can be stored in underground caves and disused mines.

Transporting gas

Before gas can be transported, its volume must be reduced by compression and cooling. Natural gas can then be carried by high-pressure pipelines, or in liquid form on specially-constructed ships. The liquid petroleum gases (LPGs), such as butane and propane, liquefy fairly easily. They can be stored and transported at normal temperatures. Liquefied natural gas (LNG), which is liquid methane, requires constant refrigeration.

▼ (main picture) A section of the 1,300-km long Trans-Alaskan Pipeline snaking across the frozen wastes of Alaska. In the northern part of the state, the pipeline is constructed above ground. This is necessary because the oil passing through is warm and the ground beneath is permanently frozen. Piping the oil through the ground would cause the permafrost to melt, leading to severe environmental damage.

▼ (inset) A team of crawler-tracked pipe-laying machines work in concert to lower a section of the Trans-Siberian Pipeline into a trench. This pipeline carries natural gas 6,000 km from Siberia into Europe.

Refining

Crude oil is of little immediate use, because the individual hydrocarbons are completely mixed together. Useful fuels and other products have to be separated from the crude oil by refining. An oil refinery operates around the clock, processing up to 200,000 barrels of oil per day.

The main refining process is that of distillation, which is based on the fact that different substances vaporize and condense at differing temperatures. Hydrocarbons with small, light molecules, for example methane and butane, are gases at room temperature. The heaviest hydrocarbons, such as asphalt, are almost solid. The liquid fuels: heating oil, diesel, petrol and paraffin, all vaporize at fairly low temperatures.

Simple distillation releases only a small amount of impure fuel. Refineries use a sophisticated process known as fractional distillation to separate crude oil into its component parts, or fractions. The process is carried out inside a hollow steel tower known as a fractionating column. In large refineries these tower more than 45 m above the ground, and contain 30-40 separate condensing plates.

After fractionation, the heavy oils that are left can still be made to produce useful fuel by cracking them. When heated under pressure, their molecules split up into lighter, more valuable hydrocarbons. The cracking process is accelerated if the hot oil is passed through catalysts such as natural and artificial clays.

The most modern refineries use molecular sieves made from certain dehydrated minerals. Depending on the final product required, the broken molecules may then be recombined into other compounds by a second catalytic process. Pumping hydrogen into the catalyst also boosts the efficiency of the cracking process.

Other techniques are also employed. Liquid petroleum gases are sometimes extracted by the absorption process, in which hydrogen is bubbled through the crude oil. The gases are then recovered by washing the hydrogen with steam. Solvents and acids are often used at the end of the refining process to remove impurities.

Refineries also produce white spirits, waxes, greases, and carbon black for printing ink. Many other products are used as feedstock (raw material) for the petrochemical industry.

Fractionating column

◀ Crude oil is heated to about 350°C before it is pumped into the bottom of the column. Oil vapour then rises up the column through a series of steel trays, each of which contains a large number of condensation traps. The trays are maintained at slightly different temperatures, gradually getting cooler towards the top of the column. Different fuels and other products condense in the trays at different heights, and are tapped off. Any gas in the crude oil passes out of the top of the column, and is piped to a gas separation plant.

▶ The lights of an oil refinery glow against the night sky. An oil refinery involves several complex processes. After fractionating, some of the heavier oils are passed to the catalytic cracking plant to be broken into lighter grades. Sulphur may be removed from diesel fuel. The heavier fractions may be further processed, and a vacuum distillation plant produces lubricating oil and paraffin wax.

Nuclear power

Spot facts

- Five tonnes of uranium fuel will produce the same amount of useful energy as 125,000 tonnes of coal or 500,000 barrels of oil.

- Fast, or breeder, reactors actually produce more fuel than they use.

- Some waste products produced by nuclear power stations (such as plutonium) will continue to emit dangerous radioactive particles for many thousands of years.

- The first nuclear reactor was built by a team under the direction of US physicist Enrico Fermi in Chicago in 1942.

Uranium is the rarest of all naturally-occurring "fuels", and it is also the most powerful. Inside a nuclear reactor, uranium can be made to release energy from the very heart of each atom. Most of this energy is in the form of useful heat. Nuclear power stations use only small amounts of uranium fuel, but produce large quantities of electricity.

Unfortunately, uranium is also our most potentially dangerous fuel. As well as heat, uranium emits potentially harmful radiations. Many people believe that nuclear power production presents a serious threat to planet Earth. In some countries, the subject of nuclear energy is now highly controversial.

► The control room at the Calder Hall nuclear power station in Britain. Calder Hall was the first commercial nuclear reactor, and it commenced operation in 1956. Today there are about 280 nuclear power stations located in some 25 different countries.

Safe energy?

The first experimental nuclear power plant started operating in the United States in 1951. Initially, there was considerable enthusiasm for this new source of energy. Nuclear power promised to supply the world with large quantities of clean, cheap electricity, especially in countries that lacked reserves of coal and oil. By the early 1960s, more than 100 nuclear power stations had been built. Developing nations were especially eager to acquire this new technology. Today, however, a very large question mark hangs over the nuclear power industry.

The great advantage of nuclear energy is that it uses very little fuel. The great disadvantage of nuclear energy is that it produces high levels of harmful radiation. In 1986, an accident caused an explosion at the Chernobyl nuclear power station in Russia. The explosion created a cloud of radioactive material that contaminated land and therefore food supplies over large areas of Russia and Europe.

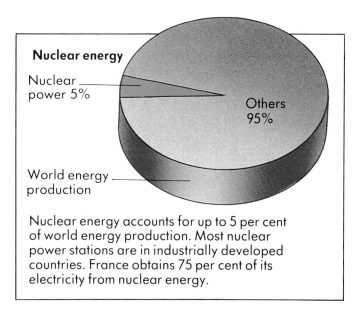

Nuclear energy

Nuclear power 5%

Others 95%

World energy production

Nuclear energy accounts for up to 5 per cent of world energy production. Most nuclear power stations are in industrially developed countries. France obtains 75 per cent of its electricity from nuclear energy.

▼ The nuclear power station at Three Mile Island, Pennsylvania,USA. In 1979, an accident caused the core of the reactor to overheat so much that it began to melt (inset). If the core had melted down completely, huge amounts of radioactivity could have been released, threatening the lives of thousands.

How it works

Nuclear energy is the energy released during the fission, or splitting, of uranium atoms. As well as releasing energy, the fission of a uranium atom also releases neutrons. Some of these strike other uranium atoms, causing them to split, thus releasing more energy and more neutrons. This process is known as a chain reaction. Uranium is the only element which occurs naturally and in which a chain reaction can take place.

Once it has started, a chain reaction tends to accelerate until all the uranium is consumed. Under particular circumstances the chain reaction can be made to happen almost instantaneously. This produces the awesome destructive power of an atomic bomb. Huge amounts of energy are released, but it cannot be put to any constructive purpose.

A nuclear reactor is a device for producing a slow, controlled chain reaction. The energy that is produced is released at useful levels over long periods of time.

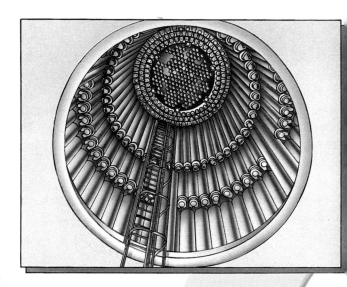

▲ Uranium fuel is loaded into a large number of cylindrical metal containers known as fuel rods. These are then packed closely together to form the core of the reactor. The shape of the core varies with different designs of reactor.

Inside the atom

An atom consists of a nucleus surrounded by shells of orbiting electrons. The nucleus itself is composed of protons and neutrons, held together by an incredibly strong force. When an atom splits, some of this force is converted into very large amounts of energy.

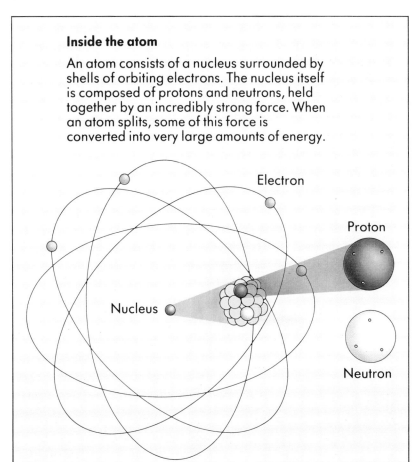

Electron

Proton

Nucleus

Neutron

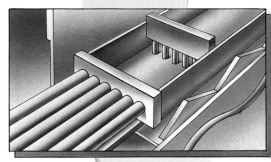

▲ The ore has to be refined in order to produce uranium fuel, which is shaped into thin rods or compressed into pellets.

▼ Mining uranium ore. Even good-quality ore may contain as little as 1-2 per cent uranium. The largest deposits are in North America.

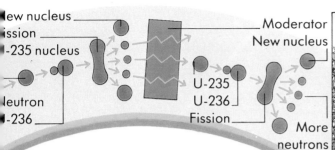

▲ A chain reaction starts with an atom of uranium being struck by a stray neutron. Fission then produces more neutrons, which enable the chain reaction to proceed. The moderator helps control the speed of the chain reaction.

▲ The dangers of radioactivity mean that great care must be taken when transporting nuclear fuel. Special railway trucks are often used. These are designed to withstand a crash at speeds of up to 150 km/h.

All forms of radioactive waste, including the clothing worn by workers, must be carefully sealed and stored. Waste with only a small amount of radioactivity is often stored in steel drums.

▼ Using nuclear fuel requires a cycle of different processes. Uranium must be processed before it can be loaded into a reactor. After use, the fuel must be reprocessed for safe disposal.

◄ Highly radioactive waste must be treated with the utmost care. At this French installation, nuclear waste is being sealed into glass blocks. This reduces the risk of a leakage of radioactivity into the environment.

Reactors

A nuclear reactor has three basic components: a core, a coolant system and a containment. The core produces heat, and the coolant system carries the heat away from the reactor. Most coolant systems operate under high pressure, and the whole reactor is therefore encased in a strong reactor vessel. The containment is an outer covering, usually made of reinforced concrete, that prevents radiation escaping.

The core consists of the uranium fuel rods arranged within a moderator. The moderator serves to slow down neutrons, because slower neutrons bring about fission more readily. The intensity of the chain reaction can be adjusted by a series of control rods made from substances that absorb neutrons. Lowering the control rods causes the chain reaction to slow down. Raising them speeds it up.

The different types of nuclear reactor are designed to make use of different grades of uranium fuel. Natural uranium metal can only be used as a fuel if it is surrounded by an extremely efficient moderator, such as graphite. The uranium is formed into fuel elements, and as many as 30,000 may be stacked into a graphite core measuring up to 14 m high. Such reactors have a coolant system that uses high-pressure carbon dioxide gas, and are usually known as gas-cooled reactors.

The majority of reactors currently in use run on uranium fuel which has been improved by the process of enrichment. Instead of uranium metal, they use a compound known as uranium dioxide. Reactors that run on enriched fuel can use ordinary water, both as a moderator and as a coolant.

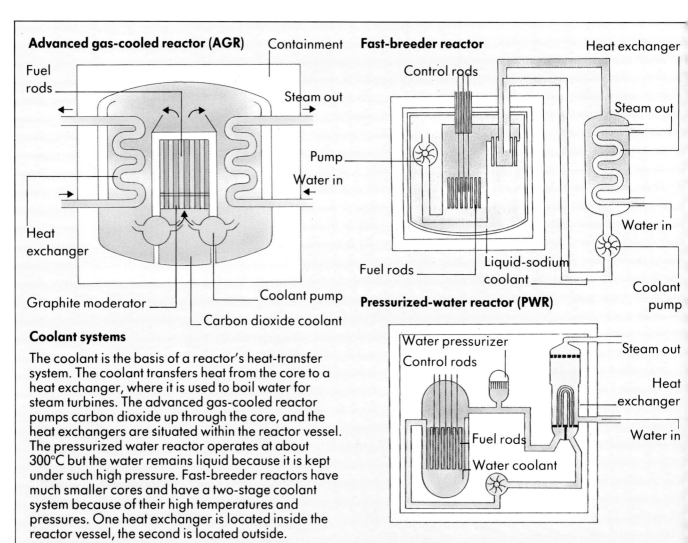

Advanced gas-cooled reactor (AGR) — Containment, Fuel rods, Steam out, Water in, Heat exchanger, Graphite moderator, Coolant pump, Carbon dioxide coolant

Fast-breeder reactor — Control rods, Heat exchanger, Steam out, Pump, Water in, Fuel rods, Liquid-sodium coolant, Coolant pump

Pressurized-water reactor (PWR) — Water pressurizer, Control rods, Steam out, Heat exchanger, Fuel rods, Water in, Water coolant

Coolant systems

The coolant is the basis of a reactor's heat-transfer system. The coolant transfers heat from the core to a heat exchanger, where it is used to boil water for steam turbines. The advanced gas-cooled reactor pumps carbon dioxide up through the core, and the heat exchangers are situated within the reactor vessel. The pressurized water reactor operates at about 300°C but the water remains liquid because it is kept under such high pressure. Fast-breeder reactors have much smaller cores and have a two-stage coolant system because of their high temperatures and pressures. One heat exchanger is located inside the reactor vessel, the second is located outside.

Most water-cooled reactors use water at over 00 times atmospheric pressure, and are known s pressurized-water reactors (PWR). Other esigns make use of boiling water as a coolant.

If uranium fuel is very highly enriched, it can e used in reactors that do not need a noderator. This type of reactor is known as a ast reactor. Fast reactors can also make use of lutonium, an element extracted from depleted uel. One major advantage of fast reactors is hat they can be used to "breed" more lutonium from depleted uranium fuel. For this eason they are often called breeder reactors.

Fast reactors operate at higher temperatures han other reactor types, and produce energy nore efficiently. There are several designs, and ll of them use liquid sodium as a coolant.

The chart shows the electricity generating capacity f nuclear power stations ordered by European ountries during the period 1956-85. Nuclear power ecame most popular when oil prices rose during the 970s. Since the accident at Three Mile Island in 1979, uclear energy has undergone a worldwide decline in opularity. This is clearly indicated by the number of ew reactors ordered in Europe after 1980.

Hands off

Even small doses of radiation can be harmful to human health. Workers at nuclear power stations take every precaution to prevent their exposure to radiation. Inside the reactor building, workers wear heavy protective suits lined with radiation shielding. Delicate operations, such as removing depleted fuel rods, are usually carried out by remote control from behind heavily shielded walls.

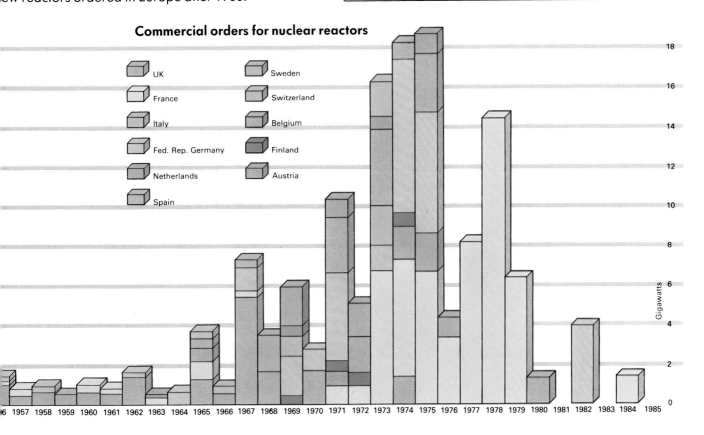

Commercial orders for nuclear reactors

UK
France
Italy
Fed. Rep. Germany
Netherlands
Spain
Sweden
Switzerland
Belgium
Finland
Austria

Gigawatts

6 1957 1958 1959 1960 1961 1962 1963 1964 1965 1966 1967 1968 1969 1970 1971 1972 1973 1974 1975 1976 1977 1978 1979 1980 1981 1982 1983 1984 1985

Solar energy

The Sun represents an inexhaustible source of free energy. Most buildings already make some use of passive solar heating, and in many countries the Sun's energy is actively collected to provide hot water for household purposes.

The main drawback with solar energy is that it produces only low temperatures under natural conditions. In order to produce useful quantities of electricity from solar energy, the heat energy in sunlight must be collected over a large area and concentrated at a single point. In countries with suitable climates, experimental solar-energy power stations are in operation.

► Located about 150 million km away, the Sun is a huge nuclear furnace that radiates vast quantities of energy into space in all directions. Only a very small proportion (about a thousand millionth) of that energy reaches Earth.

Sun power

Solar energy dwarfs all our other energy sources. In less than one hour, the Earth receives energy from the Sun that is equivalent to the world's total energy output from other sources during an entire year.

Most of the Sun's energy is reflected back into space or is absorbed by the atmosphere. However, sunlight still reaches the Earth's surface in usable quantities. On a summer's day in Britain, for example, the energy falling on one square metre of sunlit ground is equivalent to ten 100-watt light bulbs.

Sunlight provides a constant source of energy for the Earth as a whole, but it is not evenly distributed over the planet's surface. Solar energy can only be exploited where and when the sun is shining. Usually this means countries with hot climates and clear skies. Even in cold northerly countries, however, solar energy can still be very useful.

The energy in sunlight can most easily be exploited in the form of direct heat. Rooms can be heated simply by letting the Sun shine in freely. Higher temperatures, needed to provide domestic hot water, require the active technology of solar collection panels.

Sunlight can also be converted directly into electricity using solar cells. At present, these are mainly used on Earth in calculators and watches that consume only small amounts of electricity. But larger solar-powered devices also work: a solar-powered aircraft has flown between Britain and France; and solar-powered cars have been built in several countries.

▼ Some 30 per cent of the Sun's energy that reaches Earth is reflected back into space by the atmosphere. Virtually all of the remaining 70 per cent is absorbed by the atmosphere, where it powers the water cycle. Direct heating of the Earth's surface, which causes winds and currents, accounts for less than 1 per cent.

Solar energy

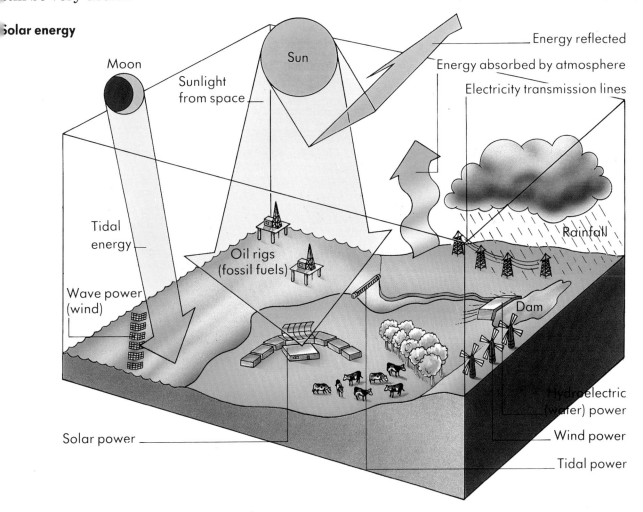

At home

All houses and other buildings already make use of solar heating from sunlight shining on walls and rooftops, and through windows. Even in countries which have cool, cloudy climates, houses obtain as much as 20 per cent of their space heating (room heating) requirements from the Sun. By incorporating passive solar technology, such as sloping windows and trombe walls, this can be boosted up to 80 per cent. This sort of heating is known as solar gain. Houses that are designed to make maximum use of solar gain are usually well insulated in order to keep heat loss to a minimum.

Producing domestic hot water from the Sun requires an active solar collector. The commonest type is the flat-plate collector, which consists of a coil of water-filled hosepipe inside a sealed glass-topped box. Black pipe is used for the coil because dark-coloured surfaces absorb heat better than lighter ones. The sealed box acts in the same way as double glazing, and reduces heat loss. The water in the pipe is connected to a closed system, and heat is transferred through another coil to a hot-water cylinder. This is more efficient than using the Sun-warmed water directly from the pipe.

Millions of these roof-top solar collectors are now in use worldwide, particularly in the countries around the Mediterranean Sea.

▼ This British house makes good use of solar gain. Large sloping windows are the simplest form of solar technology. A sloping surface can receive up to 10 per cent more solar energy than a vertical one. This principle is used in many solar-energy devices.

▲ This American house design uses light-sensitive switches to retain the heat obtained from solar gain. When the Sun is shining, the windows open and air can circulate through the house. When the Sun goes in, the switches close the windows to trap the heat.

In countries which receive less sunshine, vacuum-tube collectors can be used to supply houses with hot water. A vacuum-tube collector consists of a black metal collection plate fitted inside a sealed glass tube. A vacuum inside the tube insulates the plate against heat loss. Heat is transferred by a coolant liquid circulating within the collection plates. A typical installation may contain 20 or 30 tubes connected together.

Vacuum-tube collectors are more expensive than flat-plate collectors, but can deliver about twice as much useful energy over a year. By surrounding the tubes with curved mirrors, or by focusing the Sun's rays through lenses, higher temperatures and greater efficiency can be achieved.

Active and passive

The flat-plate collector is a form of active solar technology. The Sun's energy is used to heat water, and that heat is then transferred to a separate supply of water. A trombe wall is a form of passive technology that makes greater use of solar gain. Sunlight shining through the glass outer wall is absorbed by the dark-coloured inner wall. Convection currents circulate warm air into the room, and draw cold air out. The inner wall also radiates heat into the room.

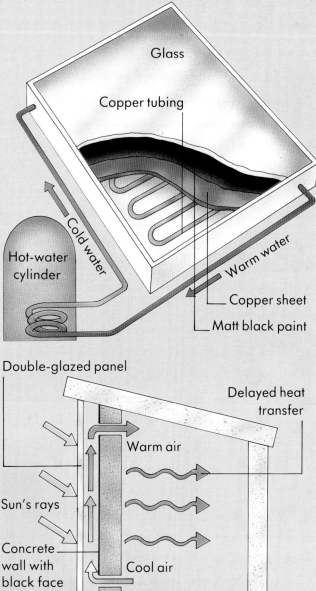

33

Solar electricity

Producing useful quantities of electricity from solar energy requires a very large-scale installation. The most widely-adopted design is that of the solar field. This is already being used in several countries including Australia, Japan, Spain, Italy and the USA.

A solar field consists of many rows of individual solar collectors. These are connected to a central heat exchanger that produces steam to drive an electric generator. The collectors are normally surrounded by curved reflectors, and are made even more efficient by the process of Sun-tracking. Each collector is mounted so that it can be swivelled and tilted to be always facing directly at the Sun. Throughout the day, the position of the collectors are constantly adjusted by small computer-controlled motors.

The main disadvantage with the solar field is that heat energy is lost during the transfer from the collectors to the central heat exchanger. One solution to this problem is to concentrate the Sun's heat into a central collection point by using a circular field containing thousands of separate mirrors. The first central collection systems were experimental solar furnaces that could reach temperatures above 3,000°C. During the last ten years, however, the first central collection power towers have begun operating. The Sun's rays are focused at the top of the power tower, and heat is collected by a series of black-coloured pipes containing liquid sodium. Heat exchangers at the base of the tower are connected to boilers that produce steam to drive generators.

Photo-voltaic cells can also be used to produce large quantities of electricity, but at present the process is too expensive to be practical. They are more efficient in space than on Earth.

▶ The world's largest power tower at Barstow, California, USA. The tower itself stands about 90 m tall, and the field of mirrors covers some 90,000 square metres.

Solar cells

A solar cell, often called a photovoltaic (PV) cell, converts the energy in sunlight directly into electricity. An individual cell consists of two thin slices of silicon crystal sandwiched between two layers of metal. The top layer of metal is in the form of a grid so that sunlight can reach the upper side of the silicon. The two slices of silicon contain slightly different amounts of impurities, causing them to have different electrical states. Sunlight falling on the upper slice causes electrons to flow into it from the lower slice. This creates an electrical current that flows through the metal contacts. The photo shows panels of solar cells mounted on a research satellite. In space, the cells will receive the full strength of the Sun's rays, and will be able to operate at maximum efficiency. On the Earth's surface, however, even strong sunlight has had most of the energy filtered from it by the atmosphere.

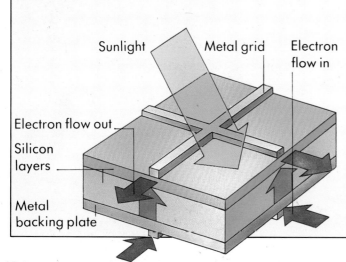

Sunlight   Metal grid   Electron flow in

Electron flow out

Silicon layers

Metal backing plate

Energy from the elements

► Waves crashing ashore are a constant reminder of the energy that the seas and oceans contain. Our coastlines offer tremendous potential for the future, but wave-power devices are still at the scale-model stage. At present, the cost of building full-sized machines is far too high to be practicable.

Our planet is rich in natural sources of energy. Water power, wind power and wave power provide further opportunities to use the energy of the Sun. Solar heat powers the water cycle, which provides rainfall and running water. Uneven heating of the Earth's surface causes the winds to blow, and at sea the wind creates waves. The daily rise and fall of the tides, however, is caused by gravitational effect of the Moon.

The motion of water, wind, waves and tides can all be harnessed by machines, with varying degrees of success. Geothermal energy is the heat energy found in rocks deep below our planet's surface. This source of energy can be used more directly.

Nature's power

Nearly all of nature's power that we harness comes in the form of movement. It is largely a case of converting one sort of movement into another. The movement of running water and the rushing wind is converted into rotation by machines based on the wheel.

A waterwheel is placed edge-on into a flow of water. The wheel is turned by the force of the flow against blades set across the wheel's rim.

In a traditional windmill, the wheel takes the form of a number of angled blades, or sails, which are placed face on to the wind. A windmill turns because the wind is deflected by the angled blades as it flows through the wheel.

Waterwheels and windmills have been in widespread use for at least 2,000 years. Since Roman times they have provided useful energy for milling grains for flour, or for pumping water for irrigation and drainage. At the beginning of the Industrial Revolution, water power provided most of the energy that drove the spinning wheels and other machinery in the first factories.

During the last 100 years, the energy conversion process has been taken one step further. Water and wind power are now used to drive turbines. These in turn are used to generate energy in the form of electricity.

► Traditional windmills provided a steady source of low-speed rotation that was very useful for certain tasks such as grinding corn or pumping water.

▼ An ancient waterwheel in Syria, possibly dating from Roman times. Waterwheels could be almost any size, but until the 1700s the materials used were very weak.

Water power

Water is the most useful source of natural power because it is the easiest to control. Running water can be channelled along sluices and through pipes. More importantly, a river can be blocked by a dam, creating a reservoir that can store huge quantities of water. Water from the reservoir can then be released as and when it is required.

Water power is harnessed to generate electricity in hydroelectric power (HEP) stations. These are usually situated at the base of a large dam. The best locations for HEP projects are the narrow, steep-sided river valleys found in mountainous areas. A dam across such a valley can create a reservoir more than 100 km long. Large-scale HEP projects may involve more than a simple dam and reservoir. In the Snowy Mountains of Australia, the waters of the Snowy River have been diverted by a series of underground tunnels to some 16 HEP stations.

Water power can also be used to store surplus energy from other power stations. This is carried out in what are known as pumped-storage HEP schemes. These use two separate reservoirs at different levels.

During normal operation, water from the upper reservoir is used to drive turbines to produce electricity. After passing through the turbines, the water is stored in the lower reservoir. Whenever there is a surplus of electricity, it is used to pump water from the lower reservoir back up into the higher one. Demand for electricity is at its highest during the day. This means that, in most stations, pumping is often done at night.

▼ Construction workers inside the tunnels at a HEP station. The worker on the right is in the main water-supply tunnel. The worker on the left is standing at the mouth of an intake pipe leading to a turbine.

Hydroelectricity

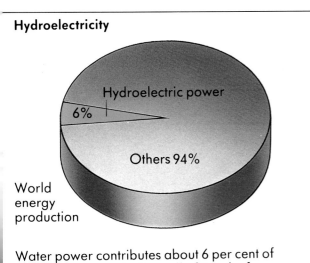

Hydroelectric power

6%

Others 94%

World
energy
production

Water power contributes about 6 per cent of
world energy production, all of it in the form
of hydroelectric power. Large HEP schemes
supply about one-quarter of the world's
electricity. Compared with water power,
none of the other sources of natural energy
significantly contribute to world output.

▼ Dams are normally curved as this gives them
greater strength. The level of water in the dam is
carefully monitored, and excess water is diverted
down the spillway. The main water intakes, which are
called the penstocks, are usually located about
midway down the dam. This enables the turbines to
operate even if the water level in the reservoir drops
below normal. In this illustration, the turbines are
mounted with a vertical axis, and each drives a
separate generator, which is located directly above
the turbine.

Hydroelectric power scheme

Reservoir

Penstocks

Dam wall

Spillway

Valley sides

Hydroelectric power plant

Turbines

Generators

Wind power

Unlike water, the wind cannot be controlled or stored. Wind power must be exploited where and when it occurs naturally. Until very recently, the wind was mainly used to drive small pumps for agricultural purposes.

The amount of power produced by the wind increases as the cube of its velocity. This means that a doubling of the wind speed produces eight times as much power. In general, wind speeds increase with altitude. At 10 m above the Earth's surface, the wind speed is about 20 per cent greater than at ground level. At 60 m up, velocities may be 50 per cent greater.

Traditional windmills were designed to operate at fairly low wind speeds. The materials they were made from (wood and cloth) were not strong enough to withstand high winds.

Modern windmills, which are usually called wind turbines, are designed to operate at much higher velocities. As a result, they produce far more power, and can be used to generate electricity. There are two main types of wind turbine. The horizontal-axis turbine has the same basic layout as a traditional windmill. Instead of sails, it has a rotor shaped like an aeroplane propeller.

▼ Small wind turbines are used throughout the world to pump water and generate small amounts of electricity, particularly on farms. The commonest design uses a rotor consisting of a large number of metal vanes. The rotor turns on a horizontal axis. The whole of the turbine assembly is on a swivel mounting so that it can be turned into the wind by the attached rudder.

▶ A wind farm in California, USA, consisting of many rows of small Darreius wind turbines. Darreius turbines are easily recognizable by their distinctive shape, and can operate in wind coming from any direction. This particular wind farm is situated in a high mountain pass, where the winds are unusually strong and steady. Careful siting is the key to wind farming.

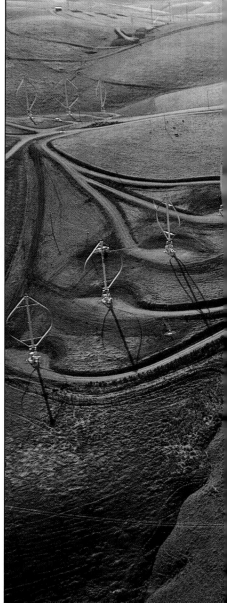

A vertical-axis wind turbine rotates on a shaft that is vertical to the ground. It normally has only two blades, mounted vertically at each end of a horizontal rotor.

The Darreius wind turbine is an advanced vertical-axis design that uses two curved blades. There is no separate rotor, and the blades are attached at each end of the shaft.

Wind turbines of both basic types are now in operation in many countries throughout the world. The largest ones are more than 100 m tall. At full speed, the tips of the blades travel at up to 400 km/h.

Wind turbines are positioned wherever the winds are strongest, and are often located on hills and clifftops. As with solar power, there are two main approaches to the large-scale use of wind power. A wind farm is a large area of land containing many small wind turbines, up to 30 m tall. Each of these contains a separate electrical generator. The other approach is to build just one or two very large turbines at each location. Taking maximum advantage of wind power may mean building wind farms offshore, where wind speeds are generally higher than over land.

Geothermal power

The Earth's crust is the thin, solid outer layer of our planet. Below about 30 km, heat from natural radioactivity is sufficient to keep rock in a molten state. The temperature rises steadily with depth, generally about 30°C for every 1,000 m of depth. In areas of volcanic activity, this can increase to 80°C per 1,000 m, and higher temperatures occur much closer to the surface.

In a few rare instances, in the USA, Japan and Italy, this heat boils underground water, which rises to the surface as dry steam. This steam can be trapped and used to drive turbines. In California, the Geysers power station has been built on top of a vast underground reservoir of dry steam. When operating at full capacity, the Geysers power station supplies nearly all the electricity required by the city of San Francisco.

In most cases, superheated water remains trapped underground. When brought to the surface by wells, the water boils and the steam is used by turbines. Several countries, as far apart as Mexico and the Philippines, already produce electricity in this way.

Low-temperature geothermal heat has been used for thousands of years in public baths and health spas. In some parts of the world, hot water from volcanic springs and geysers is now a major source of domestic heating. In Iceland more than two-thirds of the population now heat their homes with natural hot water. Other countries that make use of geothermal heating include the USA, Russia, China, Japan, France, New Zealand and Hungary.

Even when there is no naturally-occurring underground water of suitable temperature, geothermal energy can still be harnessed. Hot dry rocks may be used soon in many countries as a huge underground boiler.

▼ (right) The Geysers geothermal power station in California, USA, supplies electricity to a city of half a million people. (left) This design is for a power station producing electricity from hot dry rocks. Two wells are drilled some distance apart, one deeper than the other. The surrounding rock is then fractured with explosives to produce a large number of heat transfer surfaces. Cold water is pumped down the deeper well into the fissured rock, where it boils. Steam is tapped off by means of the other well.

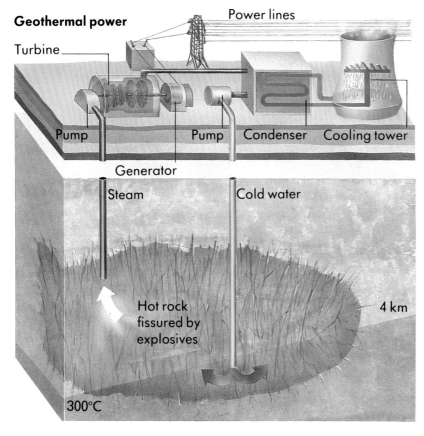

Geothermal power

Power lines

Turbine

Pump Pump Condenser Cooling tower

Generator

Steam Cold water

Hot rock fissured by explosives

4 km

300°C

Tidal and wave power

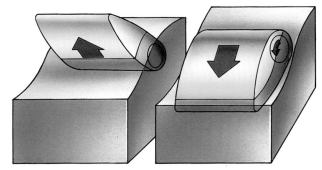

◄ A tidal-power barrage across the estuary of the River Rance in France. At 750 m long, the barrage forms the world's largest tidal-power station and contains 24 turbines, which can operate when the tide is flowing in either direction.

▼ Wave energy converters will need to be very large. (1) The Salter duck uses a string of floating ducks hinged on a common shaft; a full-sized duck would measure 25 m across.(2) A development of the air-bag principle. The motion of the wave pumps air from one side of the converter to the other. The estimated length is 250 m. (3) Each wave-contouring raft would cover at least 5,000 square metres.

1 Salter duck

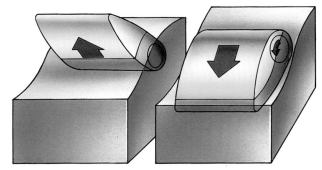

2 Air-bag device

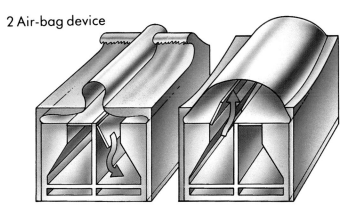

3 Wave-contouring raft

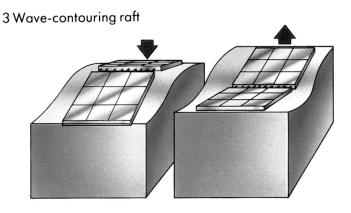

When the motion of the tides is channelled by a natural feature such as a river estuary, it produces a very strong flow of water. The power of the tides can then be harnessed by building a barrage fitted with turbines across the tidal flow. Tidal-power barrages have been built in France, Russia and China.

The ceaseless up-and-down motion of ocean waves also represents a potentially valuable source of energy. A number of wave-power devices have been invented and tested as models, but none of them yet operate.

There are two basic approaches to wave power. The simplest designs place a line of wave-energy converters across the path of incoming waves. The energy converters float on the surface and consist of two sections hinged together. The motion of the waves operates the hinge, which powers pumps that drive turbines.

Other designs place the energy converter edge-on to the waves. The converters contain a number of air bags. As the wave travels along the converter, it squeezes the bags and forces air through turbines.

Glossary

anthracite The best quality coal. A hard black substance containing at least 86 per cent solid carbon. Anthracite gives off little smoke when burned, and is mainly used in domestic fires.

anticline Dome-shaped formation of underground rock strata in which oil and natural gas often accumulate. About 80 per cent of world oil production comes from anticlines.

atom Smallest individual unit of an element, that consists of a nucleus surrounded by one or more orbiting electrons.

barrage Artificial barrier, usually built of stone or concrete, across a river or an estuary.

bituminous coal The most widely distributed form of coal, consisting mainly of solid carbon, but also containing significant quantities of coal tar and gas.

brown coal Low-grade coal that is often soft enough to be crumbled between the fingers, and which is mined in some countries for use in power stations.

carbonization Process by which dead plant material turns to carbon. The term is usually applied to the formation of coal through the action of heat and pressure within the Earth's crust.

catalyst Any substance that enables a chemical reaction to take place, or which speeds up a chemical reaction, but which is not itself changed by the reaction.

chain reaction Continuous process in which the atoms of uranium split into smaller atoms releasing large quantities of heat energy.

charcoal Black crumbly substance, consisting almost entirely of carbon, that is made by burning wood in the absence of oxygen.

Christmas tree System of vales at the top of a many oil wells, and which is used to regulate the pressure of the oil reaching the surface.

coalface That part of a coal seam which is being worked in an underground mine.

coal tar Thick, sticky liquid that can be extracted from coal, and which contains many useful chemicals.

coke Coal which has been baked in an oven to remove any gas and coal tar. Coke gives off little smoke when burned and is mainly used by industry and power stations.

containment Thick layer of reinforced concrete that surrounds a nuclear reactor as a safety precaution to prevent the escape of harmful radioactivity.

core Central part of a nuclear reactor in which a chain reaction takes place. Consists of uranium fuel rods, a moderator and control rods.

cracking Process used in the refining of crude oil, in which large hydrocarbon molecules are broken down into smaller ones.

Darreius turbine Type of vertical-axis wind turbine with curved blades that are attached to the rotor at each end.

decomposition Process by which dead plant and animal material is broken down by the action of bacteria and other microorganisms.

enrichment Process that increases the ability of uranium to sustain a chain reaction, and which therefore makes it a more useful and valuable fuel.

fast-breeder reactor Type of reactor that does not require a moderator, and which can be used to create plutonium from depleted uranium fuel.

fission Process by which a large atom splits into two smaller atoms, releasing energy.

flat-plate collector Simple device for collecting solar energy that consists of a water-filled coil behind a glass cover. Flat-plate collectors are normally used for domestic hot water and are usually installed on roof-tops.

fossil Any physical remains of ancient life. Most fossils are just impressions in stone; only under special circumstances is any organic material preserved.

fractional distillation Basic process of oil refining by which the different hydrocarbons are separated out at different temperatures inside a hollow metal column.

fuel rods Long metal cylinders into which uranium fuel is placed before it is loaded into a nuclear reactor.

gallery Side-tunnel in an underground mine, normally dug at right angles to the main tunnel.

geothermal Relating to heat energy within the Earth's crust caused by natural radioactivity.

graphite Naturally-occurring form of pure carbon.

heat exchanger Device used to transfer heat energy from one fluid to another, but without them coming into direct physical contact.

hydrocarbons Large group of chemical compounds the molecules of which consist almost entirely of hydrogen and carbon atoms. Crude oil contains thousands of different hydrocarbons and is the main source of these substances.

hydroelectric power Electricity that has been generated by using the energy in moving water.

impermeable Waterproof. The term is normally applied to rocks that do not permit water to pass through them.

insulation Any substance which is

used to prevent the unwanted transfer of energy. Heat insulation keeps things hot or cold; electrical insulation confines the flow of electricity.

kerogen Partially-decomposed plant and animal material from which oil is formed by heat and pressure within the Earth's crust.

lignite Lowest grade of coal; a brown crumbly substance mainly burned in power stations.

liquid petroleum gas Collective name for hydrocarbons such as butane and pentane which are gases at normal temperature and pressure, but which are easily liquefied for storage.

longwall Method of underground mining in which coal is taken from a seam along the entire side of a gallery. As the coal face moves back, the roof of the gallery is allowed to collapse.

methane The lightest hydrocarbon and the main constituent of natural gas.

migration (of oil and gas) Process by which oil and gas tend to move from one location to another within the Earth's crust.

moderator Substance used in the core of a reactor to reflect neutrons back into uranium fuel in order that a chain reaction can take place.

molecule Smallest unit of a particular substance consisting of a characteristic arrangement of atoms.

neutron One of the two types of sub-atomic particle (the other being a proton) that make up the nucleus of atoms.

nuclear Relating to an atomic nucleus. The term is often used to refer to the production of energy by means of a chain reaction.

nucleus Central part of an atom consisting of protons and neutrons.

oil shale Type of oil deposit in which crude oil is trapped within a fine-grained rock, and can only be removed with great difficulty.

opencast mining Simplest form of surface mining, in which coal is removed from a single large hole that has been dug down to the seam.

overburden Rocks and soil covering a coal seam that lies just below the surface.

peat Waterlogged and partially-decomposed plant material that is the first stage in the formation of coal. In some parts of the world, dried peat is used as a fuel.

penstocks Water inlets in the face of a dam that channel water to the turbines.

permeable Describes any substance that allows water to pass through it. The term is usually applied to rock.

photovoltaic cell Device that produces small amounts of electrical current when exposed to sunlight. Often called a solar cell.

plutonium Artificial element that does not occur naturally, but is produced inside nuclear reactors.

pollution Unnatural presence of any substance in the environment, usually with harmful effects.

power tower Type of central-collection system for producing electricity from solar energy. A large number of mirrors reflect the Sun's rays at the top of the tower, producing enough heat to boil water for turbines.

pumped storage Method of indirectly storing electricity. Surplus electrical power is used to pump water uphill to a reservoir. When additional electricity is required, the water is allowed to flow downhill to drive turbines.

radioactivity The disintegration of atoms of certain substances, including uranium and plutonium, which emits harmful radiation.

reactor Device for producing useful quantities of heat from a chain reaction. It consists of a core, a containment, and a coolant system.

room-and-pillar Method of underground mining in which coal is removed from a seam in a series of square "rooms", with pillars of coal being left in place to support the roof.

sedimentary rock Rock formed from layers of sediment laid down at the bottom of rivers, lakes and seas.

solar gain Heat energy which buildings receive from sunlight falling on walls, roofs and windows.

strip mining Type of surface mining in which coal is removed from a series of trenches. The overburden from one trench is used to fill in the previous trench.

superheated Describes water or steam that has been heated under pressure to above 100°C.

trombe wall Simple solar heating device that can be built into houses and other buildings. A double wall, with an outer wall of glass separated from a solid inner wall by air.

turbine Any device that produces rotary motion through the action of a gas or liquid on angled blades attached to a shaft.

uranium Heaviest naturally-occurring element and the only natural source of nuclear fuel.

well-heading Process by which oil can be loaded onto a tanker directly from an undersea oil well.

whipstock Wedge-shaped attachment used for drilling oil wells at an angle.

wind turbine Windmill that is designed to generate electricity.

Index

Further Reading

Alternative Energy series (Wayland, 1990)
Discovering Energy by Frank Frazer (Longman, 1982)
Energy by Terry Jennings (Oxford University Press, 1985)
Experimenting with Energy Alan Ward (Dryad Press, 1988)
Exploring Energy Sources by Ed Catherall (Wayland, 1990)
Focus on Resources series (Wayland)
Future Energy and Resources by Robin Kerrod (Gloucester Press, 1990)
Future Sources of Energy by Mark Lambert (Wayland, 1986)
Let's Imagine Energy by Tom Johnston (Bodley Head, 1986)